Servants of the Gospel

Essays by American Bishops on Their Role as Shepherds of the Church

Foreword by Cardinal Anthony Bevilacqua
Edited by Leon J. Suprenant, Jr.

EMMAUS
ROAD
PUBLISHING

I charge you in the presence of God and of Christ Jesus who is to judge the living and the dead, and by his appearing and his kingdom: preach the word, be urgent in season and out of season, convince, rebuke, and exhort, be unfailing in patience and in teaching. For the time is coming when people will not endure sound teaching, but having itching ears they will accumulate for themselves teachers to suit their own likings, and will turn away from listening to the truth and wander into myths. As for you, always be steady, endure suffering, do the work of an evangelist, fulfil your ministry.

2 Timothy 4:1-5

Servants of the Gospel

Essays by American Bishops on Their Role as Shepherds of the Church

Foreword by Cardinal Anthony Bevilacqua
Edited by Leon J. Suprenant, Jr.

EMMAUS
ROAD
PUBLISHING

© 2000
Emmaus Road Publishing
All rights reserved.

Library of Congress catalog no. 00-100584

Published by
Emmaus Road Publishing
a division of
Catholics United for the Faith, Inc.
827 North Fourth Street
Steubenville, Ohio 43952
(800) 398-5470

CNS cover photo by Autro Mari
Cover design and layout by
Beth Hart

Published in the United States of America
ISBN 0-9663223-6-3

Contents

Abbreviations

The Old Testament
Gen./Genesis
Ex./Exodus
Lev./Leviticus
Num./Numbers
Deut./Deuteronomy
Josh./Joshua
Judg./Judges
Ruth/Ruth
1 Sam./1 Samuel
2 Sam./2 Samuel
1 Kings/1 Kings
2 Kings/2 Kings
1 Chron./1 Chronicles
2 Chron./2 Chronicles
Ezra/Ezra
Neh./Nehemiah
Tob./Tobit
Jud./Judith
Esther/Esther
Job/Job
Ps./Psalms
Prov./Proverbs
Eccles./Ecclesiastes
Song/Song of Solomon
Wis./Wisdom
Sir./Sirach (Ecclesiasticus)
Is./Isaiah
Jer./Jeremiah
Lam./Lamentations

Bar./Baruch
Ezek./Ezekiel
Dan./Daniel
Hos./Hosea
Joel/Joel
Amos/Amos
Obad./Obadiah
Jon./Jonah
Mic./Micah
Nahum/Nahum
Hab./Habakkuk
Zeph./Zephaniah
Hag./Haggai
Zech./Zechariah
Mal./Malachi
1 Mac./1 Maccabees
2 Mac./2 Maccabees

The New Testament
Mt./Matthew
Mk./Mark
Lk./Luke
Jn./John
Acts/Acts of the Apostles
Rom./Romans
1 Cor./1 Corinthians
2 Cor./2 Corinthians
Gal./Galatians
Eph./Ephesians

Phil./Philippians
Col./Colossians
1 Thess./1 Thessalonians
2 Thess./2 Thessalonians
1 Tim./1 Timothy
2 Tim./2 Timothy
Tit./Titus
Philem./Philemon
Heb./Hebrews
Jas./James
1 Pet./1 Peter
2 Pet./2 Peter
1 Jn./1 John
2 Jn./2 John
3 Jn./3 John
Jude/Jude
Rev./Revelation (Apocalypse)

Documents of Vatican II

SC	Constitution on the Sacred Liturgy (*Sacrosanctum Concilium*), December 4, 1963
IM	Decree on the Means of Social Communication (*Inter Mirifica*), December 4, 1963
LG	Dogmatic Constitution on the Church (*Lumen Gentium*), November 21, 1964
OE	Decree on the Catholic Eastern Churches (*Orientalium Ecclesiarum*), November 21, 1964
UR	Decree on Ecumenism (*Unitatis Redintegratio*), November 21, 1964
CD	Decree on the Pastoral Office of Bishops in the Church (*Christus Dominus*), October 28, 1965
PC	Decree on the Up-to-Date Renewal of Religious Life (*Perfectae Caritatis*), October 28, 1965

OT   Decree on the Training of Priests
(*Optatam Totius*), October 28, 1965

GE   Declaration on Christian Education
(*Gravissimum Educationis*), October 28, 1965

NA   Declaration on the Relation of the Church to Non-
Christian Religions (*Nostra Aetate*), October 28, 1965

DV   Dogmatic Constitution on Divine Revelation
(*Dei Verbum*), November 18, 1965

AA   Decree on the Apostolate of Lay People
(*Apostolicam Actuositatem*), November 18, 1965

DH   Declaration on Religious Liberty
(*Dignitatis Humanae*), December 7, 1965

AG   Decree on the Church's Missionary Activity
(*Ad Gentes Divinitus*), December 7, 1965

PO   Decree on the Ministry and Life of Priests
(*Presbyterorum Ordinis*), December 7, 1965

GS   Pastoral Constitution on the Church in the Modern
World (*Gaudium et Spes*), December 7, 1965

Catechism of the Catholic Church

Throughout the text, the *Catechism of the Catholic Church* (United States Catholic Conference–Libreria Editrice Vaticana, 1994, as revised in the 1997 Latin typical edition) will be cited simply as "Catechism."

Code of Canon Law

All quotations from the current (1983) Code of Canon Law are taken from *Code of Canon Law, Latin-English Edition*, Washington: Canon Law Society of America, copyright © 1983. Throughout the text, passages from the 1983 Code will be cited simply by reference to "canon."

Lineamenta

The *lineamenta*, or working document, for the Tenth Ordinary General Assembly of the Synod of Bishops, entitled *The Bishop: Servant of the Gospel of Jesus Christ for the Hope of the World*, will usually be referred to simply as the "*lineamenta*."

I remind you to rekindle the gift of God that is within you through the laying on of my hands; for God did not give us a spirit of timidity but a spirit of power and love and self-control. Do not be ashamed then of testifying to our Lord, nor of me his prisoner, but take your share of suffering for the gospel in the power of God (2 Tim. 1:6-8).

The words of Saint Paul to Saint Timothy are a powerful guide for all who are called to be bishops in the Church. God has entrusted bishops with an awesome responsibility to bear witness to the Gospel of Jesus Christ and to shepherd His flock. Bishops bear witness by courageously teaching the truths of our Catholic Faith in spite of all obstacles and opposition. They exercise their office as shepherd in charity and mercy, at every moment bearing in mind and heart the sanctification of the people entrusted to their care. Saint Paul reminds all bishops that the strength to accomplish their duties comes from God.

The bishop, within his own diocese, is the presence of Christ, the Good Shepherd and Teacher. In communion with our Holy Father, the Pope, and all the bishops in communion with the Apostolic See, the bishop demonstrates fidelity to the Word of God and genuine concern that authentic teaching is provided to the faithful. Today, more than ever, the faithful look to their bishops for sound doctrine. It is the obligation of the bishop to ensure that those entrusted to his care are guided by his example of fidelity to the truth and his obedience to the Holy Father, the Vicar of Christ and universal Shepherd.

It is through the bishop that the faithful come to understand and appreciate their communion with the entire Church. For these reasons, the faithful must recognize the significance of union and cooperation with their bishop. At the same time, the bishop must be solicitous for the spiritual and doctrinal welfare of his people. He must listen to their voices and respond to their needs with a shepherd's care.

Mindful of the crucial role of bishops in the Church, Pope John Paul II has called for a Synod of Bishops in 2000. The task of this Synod will be to address the life and ministry of bishops, particularly as we enter the third millennium of Christianity. At this critical and exciting time in the history of the Church, the bishops of the world will have the opportunity to reflect on their ministry of shepherding, teaching, and sanctifying the People of God and, under the guidance of our Holy Father, consider how they may evangelize and support their sisters and brothers in the next millennium.

In anticipation of this upcoming synod of bishops, *Lay Witness* magazine has requested several notable bishops of dioceses in the United States to contribute essays which explain the role of bishops in the Church. These essays, which were published in various issues of *Lay Witness* magazine, now have been compiled in a single volume. It is the hope of the publisher that this book will offer to the reader an understanding of the ministry of bishops, as well as their relationship with the clergy, religious, and lay faithful of their dioceses.

During these important days in the history of the Church, the lay faithful have been asked to collaborate with their bishops and priests in various forms of ecclesial service, such as pastoral planning. For all who participate in such initiatives, this book will prove to be a significant resource for understanding the role of bishops in the life of the Church. For this reason, I am pleased to recommend it to priests, religious and, particularly, the lay faithful, as well as to my brother bishops, for all readers will benefit from the insights provided in these essays.

Pope John Paul II, in preparing the entire Church to enter the Great Jubilee Year 2000, has observed that the third millennium will be a "new springtime" for Christianity. Joining the Holy Father, the entire Church is filled with expectation and hope that this new millennium will be a time of renewed faith and active evangelization. It is the responsibility of all the faithful— clergy, religious, and laity—to make this new springtime a reality. It is the particular mission of the bishop to build up and confirm the faithful in their responsibility by teaching the Gospel and upholding the truths of the Church. In his fidelity to this duty, the bishop will be for his people a sign of hope to whom they can look for guidance and light. This is the basic message of this volume. This is what it means to be a "Servant of the Gospel."

Cardinal Anthony Bevilacqua
Archbishop of Philadelphia
Solemnity of the Epiphany

January 2, 2000

The idea for this series of essays came to me while reading the July 15, 1998 English edition of *L'Osservatore Romano*, the official Vatican newspaper. This issue contained a document, known as a *lineamenta*, entitled *The Bishop: Servant of the Gospel of Jesus Christ for the Hope of the World*. This particular *lineamenta* is the working document for the Tenth Ordinary General Assembly of the Synod of Bishops, scheduled to take place during the Great Jubilee of the Year 2000, on the bishop's role in the Church.

This Synod will bring to a logical conclusion a series of assemblies that have examined various aspects of ecclesial life in the light of Vatican II's rich teaching on the Church. Past Synods, for example, have focused on the laity, formation of priests, and consecrated life. These Synods foster a deeper understanding and implementation of conciliar teaching, and are typically capped by a "post-synodal apostolic exhortation" by the Holy Father that synthesizes the Synod's deliberations.

As the Church prepares to reflect on the vital role of the bishop in the life of the Church, I thought the readers of *Lay Witness* magazine (1-800-MY-FAITH) would benefit from an ongoing catechesis on the subject by bishops themselves. Accordingly, I divided the *lineamenta* into ten topics and asked some American bishops to participate in this project by being guest columnists. Their generous response allowed *Lay Witness* to publish a ten-part series in 1999 that has now been brought together in this single volume.

Why is it important for the laity to reflect on the role of the bishop at this time? The Catechism reminds us that the bishop is "the visible source and foundation of unity" in his diocese (no. 886). As a successor of the apostles, he is an authentic teacher of the Christian faith "endowed with the authority of Christ" (no. 888, quoting LG 25).

In an address given on November 20, 1999, Pope John Paul II gave the following teaching on how the laity should relate to their bishops and derivatively to their priests:

> I likewise point out the attitude that the laity should have toward their bishops and priests: "To their pastors they should disclose their needs and desires with that liberty and confidence which befits children of God and brothers of Christ. . . . If the occasion arises, this should be done through the institutions established by the Church for that purpose and always with truth, courage, and prudence and with reverence and charity toward those who, by reason of their office, represent the person of Christ" (LG 37).

> Unity with the bishop is the essential and indispensable attitude of the faithful Catholic, for one cannot claim to be on the Pope's side without also standing by the bishops in communion with him. Nor can one claim to be with the bishop without standing by the head of the college.[1]

---

[1] Pope John Paul II, *Ad limina* address to German bishops (November 20, 1999) no. 7, as published in *L'Osservatore Romano* (English ed., December 8, 1999), 5-6.

A proper understanding of the complementarity of roles in the Church, particularly the relationship of the lay faithful with their pastors, is especially important today as the laity strive to take their rightful place in the life of the Church and the "new evangelization." Vatican II stressed the laity's baptismal dignity and consequent call to holiness and mission. The clericalism of past generations, whereby the faithful are encouraged to "leave everything to Father," must be rejected.

Conversely, an active, evangelizing laity cannot fail to maintain communion of mind and heart with the local Church. God saves us as a people, as a family, and not as isolated individuals (cf. LG 9). Accordingly, the laity's approach to the apostolate must be that of collaborators, not lone rangers. On this point, Catechism, no. 896 quotes Saint Ignatius of Antioch, a bishop 1,900 years ago, who wrote: "Let no one do anything concerning the Church in separation from the bishop."

My prayer for this book is that it will help foster right relationship within the Church, so that united as members of the one Body of Christ we may help foster a new springtime of fidelity and holiness in our Church and world in the new millennium.

I owe a huge debt of gratitude to all the bishops who contributed to this project, and to all the bishops who serve as advisors of Catholics United for the Faith, the lay apostolate behind this project. I'm especially grateful to Archbishop Charles J. Chaput of Denver, whose enthusiasm and encouragement convinced me to proceed with this volume. These men, truly "Servants of the Gospel," have been an inspiration to me personally and have helped our apostolate to "think with the Church" in all things.

I also want to thank the board of directors, staff, and members—past and present—of Catholics United for the Faith and Emmaus Road Publishing, whose support made this project possible. A special word of thanks goes to Curtis Martin, Philip Gray, Shannon Hughes, Ann Recznik, Jody Trupiano, Beth Hart, and Brian Germann for their assistance.

Lastly, I'm grateful to our Holy Father, Pope John Paul II, for all that he's done to "strengthen his brethren" (cf. Lk. 22:32), and for his being such a powerful "witness to hope" in our time.

Open wide the doors to Christ!

Leon J. Suprenant, Jr.
Steubenville, Ohio

Chapter One

—Be Not Afraid—
The Bishop as Messenger of Hope
by Most Rev. Charles J. Chaput, O.F.M. Cap.

Things fall apart; the centre cannot hold . . .
The best lack all conviction, while the worst
Are full of passionate intensity.

Written in 1920, only two years after the close of a terrible war, these words are from the heart of William Butler Yeats' darkly brilliant poem, "The Second Coming." Yeats sensed, as maybe only artists can, that "surely some revelation [was] at hand," and that much of the world as he knew it would be swept away by change. He was right. But not even Yeats could have known just how great and violent our century would be.

Like Yeats, Karol Wojtyla was a poet and also a playwright. Unlike Yeats, he experienced the bitter cost of this century directly. And also unlike Yeats, he was—and is— a voice of confidence in a world overwhelmed by fear. Yeats wrote from melancholy and helplessness. Wojtyla, now Pope John Paul II, speaks of "crossing the threshold of hope" and a new springtime in the coming century not just for religious faith, but for all humanity.

So much separates the lives of these two men that any connection seems unlikely. But comparing them is more than just an academic exercise. Both knew the soul of our age. Only one chose hope. And therein lies the key to understanding this Pope's entire pontificate, and especially the Synod on the role of bishops, scheduled for the Jubilee Year 2000. With the Synod still more than a year away, the Vatican issued the *lineamenta*, or preparatory document, which set the gathering's direction and tone for discussion. And the theme should surprise no one: "The Bishop: Servant of the Gospel of Jesus Christ for the Hope of the World."

Why This Topic? Why Now?

We can best answer these questions just by browsing through a newspaper any day of the week. We live in a culture which still has a memory of God, but worships at the altar of practical materialism. As a result, we are pulled between two great polar sins: *pride* in our economic, political, financial, and technological power over the world around us; and *despair* over the limits of our power and the constant threat of losing the limited power we have.

In the developed countries especially, but also throughout the world, it is a time of immense anxiety, excess, and coarsening of attitudes toward the sanctity of life. One small example: American news media recently reported that legislators in Belgium have demanded that the government should end its ban against euthanasia . . . because doctors and patients routinely ignore it anyway. This is taking place in an overwhelmingly "Catholic" nation—a nation where the standards and satisfactions of living are envied by much of the world.

To paraphrase Scripture: Without hope, the people perish. Against this culture of emptiness and self-destruction, Pope John Paul II has fixed his eye on the Great Jubilee since the day of his election over twenty years ago.

Preparing the Church to better serve God as a beacon of hope in the new millennium has always been one of his goals. To do that, he has systematically submitted every aspect of Catholic life to review and renewal in light of Vatican II—a council whose heart he knows from personal experience. As the *lineamenta* document suggests, the Synod in 2000 will conclude a profound and comprehensive review of Church life *as a communion in Christ for the evangelization and salvation of the world.*

The process began in 1987 with the Synod on the laity. It continued through 1990 and 1994 with Synods on the priesthood and consecrated life, respectively. Now it reaches completion in examining the vocation of the bishop, who "is the principle and visible source of unity in the Church entrusted to his pastoral service" (*lineamenta*, no 4; cf. Catechism, no. 886). Over the past decade, then, the Holy Father has carefully affirmed the dignity—and explained the role—of each state of life in the Church. Or to say it another way, he has put our family affairs in order, the better to accomplish the work we are all called to do, as a family of faith, in the new age before us.

Every bishop is the "father" of his local family of faith. It makes sense, therefore, that the Pope's review should finish with a reflection on the vocation of bishops, who bear a special responsibility for the mission of the Church. In that regard, the Synod's official theme is itself a small catechesis. The bishop is first of all a *servant.* His authority does not come from power, personal achievement, or popular acclaim, but from service to Someone else who confers it on him. He serves the *Gospel*, which is a message of good news and great joy. (Remember that joy is the surest sign of the presence of God. Dissension also suggests a presence . . . but of a different kind.) Moreover, it is a message rooted not in ideas, programs, or ideologies, but in a real, flesh and blood Person whom we can meet and love, *Jesus of Nazareth*. This Jesus is also the eternal *Christ*, the Anointed One, the only Son of God. Finally, the Jesus Christ proclaimed by every bishop has come to save every human being, not just a nation or sect. He is therefore *the hope of the world*. In fact, He is the only hope of the world.

Every bishop must be a messenger of hope to his people and to his culture, even when the message is unpopular. Every bishop must be, above all, a preacher, teacher, and missionary of Jesus Christ—by direct leadership and personal example. After all, the Lord did no less. Neither did the apostles, to whom bishops are the successors. "Go therefore and make disciples of all nations" (Mt. 28:19) cannot be delegated.

Renewing this missionary spirit is at the heart of the Synod in 2000. It is also the antidote to the anxiety of our age, which Yeats captured so powerfully:

Things fall apart; the centre cannot hold . . .

The Holy Father answers this despair with the Person, and the words, of Jesus Christ:

"I am the resurrection and the life; he who believes in me, though he die, yet shall he live" (Jn. 11:25).

"I came that they may have life, and have it abundantly" (Jn. 10:10).

"[Y]ou will know the truth, and the truth will make you free" (Jn. 8:32).

Yeats was right: "surely some revelation is at hand." But if we allow God to do His will through us, it may be a greater and more loving revelation than the poet could have imagined. Pope John Paul II is a centripetal man in a centrifugal age: the voice of communion and hope; a force for unity in an era of loneliness and confusion.

As his brothers in the Lord, bishops are called to the same task.

Most Rev. Charles J. Chaput, O.F.M. Cap., is the Archbishop of Denver, Colorado, and a member of the episcopal advisory council of Catholics United for the Faith.

Chapter Two

—Contemporary Challenges—
The Bishop as Herald of Hope
by Most Rev. Robert J. Carlson

Pope John Paul II recently told a gathering of American bishops that "our most urgent task is to satisfy the spiritual hunger of our times." As bishops, we must above all else proclaim the joy of living in the Lord, sharing in the life of God, and belonging to the Church of Jesus Christ. The essence of Christian hope is the light of the Resurrection, which gives meaning to our lives. Calling men and women to this joyful hope, amid modern messages of indifference, incredulity, and despair, is the primary task set before the bishop today.

One of the principal challenges in our day is *secularism*, which not only attempts to eliminate rights to religious expression, but to eradicate from human consciousness the duties of religion and the sense of the sacred. Against the falsehood and emptiness of this agenda, bishops fulfill their ministry as heralds of hope by pointing to the things of heaven, tirelessly directing the hearts and minds of his faithful toward enduring spiritual realities and the happiness to which they are called. Instilling a yearning for the countless treasures of heaven is a first necessity in this day where a deeper understanding of destiny, glory, and lasting beauty has all but vanished. Only a response centered on the rights, dignity, and eternal purpose of every person can adequately counter secularism as well as the rise of "alternative religions."

Today, more than ever, we witness *a deficient understanding of the faith* among believers. This points to the need to re-catechize people at every level. Given the paramount importance of teaching Catholic doctrine, bishops must carefully oversee the preparation of catechists, as well as the selection of textbooks and teaching methods. All instruction must be based on Scripture, tradition, liturgy, and the teaching authority of the Church. Every bishop must ensure that his diocese has strong catechetical programs that foster a deeper understanding of and love for the riches of the faith, including sacred liturgy. This is possible even in a small rural diocese like my own. Using the Rural Television Network (RDTN), we gave twenty-four hours of instruction based on the *Catechism of the Catholic Church* to more than 1,500 of our 2,000 volunteer catechists at the start of this academic year, while an additional ninety-six hours will follow over the next twelve months.

Truth and Authority

Beyond this, however, we recognize a heightened need for vigilance over *fidelity to Catholic principles* in schools and institutes that bear the Catholic name. Too many theology faculties, religious study programs, textbooks, and publications enjoy the dignity and influential power of being designated "Catholic" when they have nothing to do with true Catholic principles and call into question fundamental teachings of the Catholic faith.

We also must correct the misunderstanding generated by false teaching. Many scholars and institutes of higher education propose lofty theories that represent no more than a reflection of skeptical and relativist ideologies.

This tends to mislead young students into thinking that objective truth does not exist. This same sort of deceptive methodology characterizes the prevailing forms of dissent donned in the guise of critical thinking.

In response to these prejudices, the bishop must vigilantly oversee the staffing of Catholic educational institutions. Bishops must take great care today to see that Catholic educational structures prepare the faithful to effectively share their beliefs in our pluralistic society.

Bishops also encounter a fundamental obstacle to human liberty rooted in the *modern disdain for authority*. The attitude is symptomatic of the widespread subjectivism and individualism of our age. The Church, led by the Holy Spirit, must lead a visionless world back to the truth of fulfillment in self-giving, communion, and following God's law. Authority must be reexamined so that it may be properly understood and exercised as a service, always subordinated to the greater ends of human happiness and true freedom. Today's emphasis on selfish satisfaction has distorted the understanding of freedom, presenting it as an autonomous power of self-assertion that may be pursued even to the detriment of others. In their concern to illuminate the hearts and minds of all men, bishops must convey that it is precisely by obeying the divine law inscribed in his conscience, expressed in the teaching of the Church, and urged by the gentle voice of the Holy Spirit, that man comes to a state of true freedom in which he is the master of himself and able to relate to others with interior strength and certitude.

Bishops are called to encourage others along the pathway to freedom and challenge them to embrace perfection in Christ. In this light, the meaning of sacrifice and the Cross become transparent, and bishops become heralds of hope once more by proclaiming the essence of sacrifice as true fulfillment, not destruction.

Eyes of Faith

Confronting the countless obstacles to the moral life, in a society of consumerism and rampant hedonism, bishops must exhort, enjoin, and encourage the faithful at all times with *eschatological vision*, knowing that the Church is a pilgrim people looking for the city that is to come (cf. Heb. 13:14). More than ever, there exists a need for the interior life and a reawakened fervor for the contemplative dimension of our being. The youth are starving for meaning in their lives. Bishops must announce to them and show them that, through His Church, Christ can respond to all of their expectations.

A living testimony to the surpassing worth of the kingdom of God are the religious communities residing within the diocese. The religious state of life, however, is often misunderstood and even scoffed at today. Most Catholics are ignorant of the exalted *value of consecrated life* and of the precious treasure which those committed to the religious life are for a diocese. Bishops should not only teach the Gospel mystery of dying to self, of the worth of abandoning all things for the kingdom of God, but also foster the mutual service which exists between the faithful living in the world and those who work for Christ through the counsels of poverty, chastity, and obedience.

In opposition to today's widespread promiscuity and deviant forms of sexual behavior, bishops need to boldly dismember the myths—such as that of a "population explosion"—which falsely ground the governmental promotion of *contraception and abortion*. They especially need to redirect our attention to the prophetic message of *Humanae Vitae* and to encourage the embracing and teaching of its truth-centered, life-cherishing, and joy-giving principles at home, in school, and in our daily witness.

Fraternal charity and filial sentiments should characterize the bishop's relationship with the Roman Pontiff. The teaching of the Pope should not only be accepted, but spread, supported, and defended in every episcopal see. A bishop should *never* publicly dissent from the constant teaching of the Universal Church, nor should he foster novel ideas concerning ecclesial law without conferring with other bishops of his conference. To assert one's authority outside the boundaries of the Universal Church is to abandon the meaning of the episcopal mission, which is to serve Christ in humility for the salvation of souls.

By the example of his own obedience, the bishop manifests the humility of faith which is the foundation of all spiritual growth and sharing in the life of Christ. A person cannot properly rule others unless he has first proven himself to be an *example of obedience*. If the bishop is not faithful to the leadership of the Holy Father, why should the people in his diocese follow him? Indeed, the very cause of our justification was the obedience of the Son of God, who submitted all things to His Father, even to the point of accepting death upon the Cross.

New Evangelization

One of the most serious challenges to the flourishing of the People of God—and something that is an essential concern of the bishop—is to reach out to the many Catholics who have drifted away from the faith. The fundamental way in which the bishop fulfills his teaching office is by *evangelizing* those who do not yet believe in Christ or who have deserted the Christian faith either in theory or in practice. The bishop must be a herald of the Father's merciful love, actively seeking out and welcoming home those who are lost.

In response to the lack of "practicing" Catholics and the shortage of vocations, bishops must bear witness in faith to the tremendous gift of God made present in the *sacraments* of the Church. We must direct young people's attention to the transcendent, eternal, and divine value of worship with and in the Church, thereby fostering an appreciation of sacramental grace. It should go without saying that bishops must have utmost *concern for vocations* to the sacred hierarchy upon which the sacramental life of the community depends. They should unify every resource available to promote priestly vocations and dedicate their constant care to the overseeing of seminary formation.

It is the critical responsibility of the bishop to cultivate the worship of God and thus reawaken the overall liturgical sensitivity of the ecclesial community. We witness today a tragic absence of appreciation for the profundity of the liturgy and the significance of the liturgical life of the Church. As "the principal dispensers of the mysteries of God, it is their [the bishops'] function to control, promote, and protect the entire liturgical life of the Church entrusted to them" (cf. CD 15). Not only must the theological significance of communal prayer and the sacramental nature of the sacred rites be expounded and regularly proclaimed, but bishops must see to it that the common and public worship of their dioceses is celebrated with the greatest of dignity, that the liturgical forms and activities foster devotion, adoration, joy, and thoughtful reflection. Ideally, the cathedral church should become a model of liturgical life for the entire diocese, exemplifying the qualities of a praying community fully drawn into the unique and eternal prayer of Christ. Mindful of the cultural traditions and pastoral needs of his diocese, the bishop should seek to enrich liturgical celebration in ways that stir more deeply the spiritual sensitivity of his flock and bring forth authentic expressions of faith. By his piety and seriousness in Eucharistic celebration, the bishop shows himself to be a true high priest for his people and leads them in the act of common worship founded upon the bond of charity and empowered by the sacrifice of Christ.

The bishop, with the entire Church, must pass judgment upon the *deceitful and false messages of the age.* Illusory promises and false freedoms must be bravely attacked and substituted with the message of salvation in Christ and liberation through His Cross and Resurrection. The bishop must loudly proclaim the truth about human freedom even in the face of overwhelming political opposition. He must speak out, *directly and explicitly*, against every form of injustice which jeopardizes the transcendent value of the human person. Christians must speak out against the "culture of death" so evident in politics today with the partial-birth abortion debate and the trend toward euthanasia. If the bishop is truly the leader of his people, he should be ready to lead them, even unto death, for the sake of Christ.

As apostles of Christ, bishops are travelers in a foreign land who ceaselessly lead God's people toward their heavenly home. We must be ready to risk everything to convince an increasingly skeptical Church to embrace the treasure of orthodoxy. How can we expect the faithful to follow if we cannot lead, especially in the difficult moral decisions that Christians face in this era? Let us be willing to sacrifice all for the Gospel of Jesus Christ, which guarantees the blessings that we hope for and proves the existence of the realities that at present remain unseen (cf. Heb. 11:1).

Most Rev. Robert J. Carlson is the Bishop of Sioux Falls, South Dakota, and a member of the episcopal advisory council of Catholics United for the Faith.

Chapter Three

Authority, Service, and Communion

The Ministry of the Bishop in Relation to the Blessed Trinity

by Cardinal Francis George, O.M.I.

When Catholics say, "We believe in God," we mean our faith is in the Father, Son, and Holy Spirit. God is a Blessed Trinity; all our prayers and our teaching and our lives begin and end in the name of God, who is Father, Son, and Holy Spirit.

It is Jesus, our Savior, who introduces us to His Father and makes it possible—because we are in Him through Baptism—to call His Father our Father. "Lord, show us the Father," Philip said to Jesus, to which Jesus replied, "He who has seen me has seen the Father" (Jn. 14:8-9). To know the Father, we look at Jesus.

To know Jesus Himself, we look at the record and the witnesses. We look at and live in the tradition, both written in Holy Scripture and oral in the liturgy and teaching of the Church, which links us to Jesus in the community He left behind. In the Church, Christ's body, we receive Scripture and are told it is God's holy Word. In the Church, the risen Lord touches and shapes us through the seven sacraments, which are His own actions in our space and time. In the Church, we recognize the Lord because we live by the Spirit Jesus sends.

To know the Holy Spirit, who is always self-effacing, we look at the results, the gifts, and the fruits that bear witness to the Spirit's activity in the Church. The Spirit is wind or force; the Spirit is fire or warmth and light. The Spirit is prophetic, always pointing to Christ and keeping us in Christ's truth.

Trinitarian Life

Father, Son, and Holy Spirit are one God. Each Person of the Blessed Trinity is totally given to the others. Their "sharing" is perfect. The presence of one divine Person means the presence of all three in our lives. Each is God, yet there is only one God, because each Person is perfectly and simply a relation to the other two. God is perfect self-giving, perfect generosity. God, as Saint John says, is love (1 Jn. 4:8).

The Church is a network of relationships because she lives God's life, Trinitarian life. The Church, like the Trinity, is a communion of persons, each intrinsically related because all share the gifts Christ gives His people. The basic gift is *sanctifying grace*, which justifies us and enables us to live God's own life by freeing us from sin, healing our souls, and enabling us to act in a supernatural manner. If God's life is one of infinite generosity shared in a Trinitarian order, then so it is with the Church's life, because the Church reflects, causes, and makes visible God's life in us. The Church's life is one of grace and charisms, both institutional and personal, shared visibly in an ordered pattern called *ecclesial communion*.

The sacraments of the Church are the principal means for making this dynamic of shared gifts visible. As Saint Paul says, it is Christ who baptizes; and it is Christ who confirms and forgives and heals and unites and ordains and gives us not just His Word but His very Self in the sacrifice of the altar. Christ shares His gifts and His very Self with His people until He returns again in glory.

Representatives of Christ

In the meantime, in our time, the Church is governed apostolically, by the successors of those whom Christ first commissioned to preach the Gospel to the nations and to establish local Churches. With and under the successor of Peter, the head of the Twelve, the bishops are charged to preach Christ's truth, to celebrate Christ's sacraments, to govern and love Christ's people, and to see that all Christ's gifts are available to His people.

In each particular Church or diocese, therefore, the bishop is the visible point of reference for all those who gather in Christ's name. The bishop makes Christ's headship visible in a particular Church. He is married to his people, which is why he wears a ring. He is the shepherd of his people, which is why he carries a staff or crozier. He is the head of his people, which is why he wears a miter or crown.

Like and in God the Father, the bishop as life-giver is the source of authority in his local Church. Like and in God the Son, the bishop as servant gathers the baptized into the Eucharistic assembly and sends them on mission to transform the world. Like and in God the Holy Spirit, the bishop unites, encourages, challenges, comforts, and strengthens the people confided to his pastoral care. Since God is love, the virtue that is preeminent in the ministry of the bishop is *pastoral charity*, which regulates and informs all other virtues in his life.

The Way of Prayer

The spiritual life of the bishop reflects and strengthens his ministry. Our spiritual life—the believer's life in Christ—relates us to the Blessed Trinity internally and is visibly expressed in our prayer and works. The bishop, therefore, is most himself when he is at prayer, celebrating the Mass in his cathedral, surrounded by his priests and deacons, breaking open the Word of God for the holy People of God and bringing them with him into the sacrifice which unites us most perfectly to God through the Body and Blood of Jesus Christ. The structure and prayer of the Mass is totally Trinitarian, beginning in the name of the Father, Son, and Holy Spirit, and ending with God's blessing. The Eucharistic Prayer is prayed to the Father, through the Son, and in the Holy Spirit. After the bishop or priest makes Christ's Body and Blood present in an unbloody manner, the whole assembly offers Christ's sacrifice to the Father in the power of the Holy Spirit. Only then, visibly in Christ, do we dare to say, "Our Father" and share the first gift of the Holy Spirit—peace—before receiving the Eucharist as our food and drink.

In his personal prayer and pastoral contacts, the bishop also lives and acts in Trinitarian fashion. The Liturgy of the Hours is as Trinitarian as the Mass and the other sacraments. The bishop's prayer for his people enables him to bring their deepest concerns into the heart of God's love. His work for his people draws him into the self-sacrifice that conforms him spiritually to Christ. Because his vocation and mission in the Church are Trinitarian, so must be his personal spiritual life. But in his life with God, the bishop never lives alone. Because, as Saint Irenaeus wrote, "the bishop is in the Church and the Church is in the bishop," the bishop becomes holy only with and through his people.

The Directory for the Pastoral Ministry of Bishops reminds every bishop that he

> should combine in himself, at one and the same time, the qualities of both a brother and a father, a disciple of Christ and a teacher of the faith, a son of the Church and, in a certain way, a father of the Church, for he ministers the spiritual birth of Christians (1 Cor. 4:15).[1]

Rooted in faith and growing in love, the bishop's Trinitarian life and ministry should give hope to his people so that they can be light to the world. He is called by God to this vocation and is sustained in it by the prayers of the people. Every bishop is grateful for his vocation, but every bishop also recognizes how fragile his own cooperation with God's grace can be. The Church encourages prayers for the Pope and other bishops because without them the risk is great that the bishop will begin to go his own way and forsake the saving embrace of Father, Son, and Holy Spirit.

Cardinal Francis George, O.M.I., is the Archbishop of Chicago, Illinois.

---

[1] Vatican Congregation for Bishops, Directory for the Pastoral Ministry of Bishops *Ecclesiae Imago* (1973), no. 14.

Chapter Four

—An Apostolic Legacy—
The Bishop's Pastoral Authority
by Most Rev. James P. Keleher

"As the Father sent me so I send you" was Jesus' commission to His apostles. This apostolic mandate is the fundamental reason for the bishops' pastoral authority. It is not some historical development that occurred out of human need or from devious manipulation, but an authority based on Scripture and Tradition. It is a pastoral authority which Jesus handed on to His apostles and their successors for the sake of His body, the Church. He did so because His Church, born from His wounded side, is meant to be the perennial instrument of salvation to the nations until the end of time.

In addition to calling Timothy and Titus to a personal holiness of life, Saint Paul carefully instructed these disciples in his letters on the manifold duties of being a bishop. Above all, he exhorted them to guard the "deposit of faith" that had been handed down from Christ to the apostles and now to those shepherds who would succeed them in the local Churches of the known world (cf. 1 Tim. 6:20).

The Greek word that Paul used for the "deposit of faith" ("*paratheke*," 2 Tim. 1:14) signifies a precious treasure that has been entrusted to a faithful steward to keep carefully until the master returns to claim it. In other words, the bishop's mandate to teach and preach is not permission to create some new and appealing vision that will be attractive to contemporary tastes. No, the bishop must protect the integrity of the deposit of faith, reflect upon it, and proclaim it in its entirety to his flock.

Fidelity to the Gospel

In this sense, a bishop is to be a "conservative" in the best sense of that word—he is to conserve the precious Gospel treasure without change, and do so in the ongoing light of Catholic Tradition and not in the light of some more recent and highly imaginative theologies. He must tirelessly proclaim God's Word, calling all people to "believe, repent, and be baptized" (cf. Acts 2:38). For this is the Gospel as handed down by Christ to Peter and the apostolic college and now to their successors, the Pope and all bishops in union with him.

What are we to teach? What is at the heart of the Gospel? I feel we are duty bound to proclaim in one way or another the following: God the Father is not some distant deity but rather our creative, merciful Father who so loved the world that He sent His only begotten Son, Jesus Christ, who is truly God and also Mary's Son in the flesh. As we celebrate the 2,000th anniversary of His birth at Bethlehem, we recognize that there is no other name by which we can be saved. His love for us is shown in the Cross He endured and confirmed in His Resurrection.

Like Paul the preacher once put it for all of us: "[T]he life I now live in the flesh I live by faith in the Son of God, who loved me and gave himself for me" (Gal. 2:20). Because of the wounds of original sin, we must continue to seek to be converted, to turn to Him, to find the grace and strength to live the life He calls us to lead as His disciples. A deep, personal relationship with Jesus and ongoing conversion of heart is critical for each of us and is the true beginning of the "new evangelization" called for by the Great Jubilee of the Year 2000.

As the Father sent Jesus, so He sends the Holy Spirit upon His Church and upon each one of us to bear witness to Christ in the world. But there is a difference in the way the Holy Spirit is given to the successors of the apostles who are obliged to shepherd God's people. As the Catechism (no. 890) puts it: "It is this Magisterium's task to preserve God's people from deviations and defections and to guarantee them the objective possibility of professing the true faith without error." The Holy Spirit gives us confidence that the Church will persevere in proclaiming the truth, despite turmoil and confusion.

As a bishop, I must continually proclaim the gift Jesus has given us in the Church. The Church is the Body of Christ, and in her we find all the means needed for our salvation. To confuse the Church's institutional elements with what pertains to worldly institutions of business and government is to miss the point of the gift. At her very heart the Church is both sacrament and mystery, continually offering us the way and the means to eternal life.

In the sacraments we find our spiritual nurturing and healing. The Church offers us God's Word to be our wisdom, and she also offers us her most precious gift, the Holy Eucharist, and her most consoling remedy, the Sacrament of Reconciliation. As a successor of the apostles, the bishop is entrusted with a lofty guardianship over these spiritual treasures that guide the Family of God on its earthly pilgrimage.

Courageous Witness

In turbulent and confused times, the bishop must be willing to step forward regardless of whether his voice will be appreciated. We live in an era when human sexuality has been trivialized to such an extent that fornication and adultery are presented as the normal mode of adult behavior, and condoms are freely distributed with the naïve belief that promiscuous behavior will not lead to illegitimacy, though the opposite is clearly the result. This "contraceptive mentality" is clearly encouraging the young to experiment with sexual encounters which have negative moral, spiritual, and psychological consequences that can last a lifetime.

The prevailing morality in the Western world is clearly based on personal convenience and pleasure. It is just such an attitude that has made abortion a national tragedy and even a legally protected "right." In order to salve its conscience as 1.5 million babies are destroyed each year, this nation uses euphemisms like "reproductive freedom" to disguise what every honest person recognizes is killing an innocent child in the womb. In such a climate, the bishop must clearly stand for human life, including that of the criminal condemned to the barbaric penalty of capital punishment. No matter what the political consequences may be, the bishop's solemn duty is to continue to proclaim the Gospel of Life in the face of a culture of death.

The bishop must defend and explain the truth about the marriage act. Spouses in general no longer realize that love-giving and life-giving are intimately bound together, and that contraception necessarily introduces selfishness into the marital relationship. In all likelihood, this is a major cause for the alarming increase in our society's divorce rate.

The bishop must support traditional family life while pressure increases to recognize deviant forms of sexual unions as normal patterns of communal life. The bishop should also make it clear that cohabitation before marriage is simply wrong, even though the majority of couples may engage in it—despite the fact that it is most likely going to undermine the stability of their future married state.

As always, the bishop will be accused of having an outmoded view of human sexuality, even though it is the present moral decay that has weakened the American family. As the Holy Father recently put it during the Mass in St. Louis, "As the family goes, so goes the nation."

Bishops are not only successors in authority, but also in the apostles' manner of life, their suffering for the proclamation and spreading of the Gospel, their tender care and mercy toward the faithful entrusted to them, their defense of the weak, and their constant concern for the People of God.

Pope John Paul II has brilliantly modeled and expounded upon these principles, particularly in his concern for the little person, the economic well-being of the wage earner, peace around the globe, and his concern for justice for everyone. The bishop must be one with the Holy Father in expressing concern for the poor and oppressed, speaking out against human rights violations, such as the torture of innocent victims, the horrors of ethnic cleansing and tribal genocide, and the frequent disregard for individual, personal, and religious freedom.

So many of us in America are so well off that it is sometimes difficult for us to empathize with what the mass of humanity endures. But if the bishop is truly a shepherd who manifests tender care and mercy toward the flock entrusted to him, he cannot fail to raise these issues and mobilize his people to help alleviate human suffering at home and abroad.

Son of the Church

Despite his pastoral role, the bishop remains with all the other believers as a member of Christ's faithful. While it is true that the bishop stands before the faithful as a spiritual father acting in the name and Person of Christ, it is also true that he becomes a father precisely because he is a "son" of the Church.

For the sake of the faithful, the bishop must be both a brother and father, a disciple of Christ and a teacher of the faith, a son of the Church and, in a certain way, a father of the Church, for he ministers to the spiritual birth of Christians. It is very important for the bishop to be seen as a man who is compassionate, friendly, and open to all who approach him. As a redeemed sinner, he is always in need of the Lord's merciful grace in order to be worthy of the trust that the Lord and the Church has put in him. With this grace, the bishop can be an ambassador of hope to his flock.

Most Rev. James P. Keleher is the Archbishop of Kansas City, Kansas, and a member of the episcopal advisory council of Catholics United for the Faith.

Chapter Five

—Called to Be Shepherds—
The Ministry of the Bishop
in Relation to the Lay Faithful
by Most Rev. Thomas J. Tobin

"Why do you carry that big cane?" is a question the children invariably ask whenever I visit one of the elementary schools of my diocese. The question gives me the opportunity to explain the crosier, the bishop's pastoral staff, and to speak about what it means to be a spiritual shepherd in the image of Jesus the Good Shepherd.

The image of the crosier also came to mind as I reflected on the topic, "The Ministry of the Bishop in Relation to the Lay Faithful," one of the topics for discussion at the forthcoming Synod of Bishops. More about the crosier in a moment, but first some background concerning this Synod of Bishops about bishops.

The Tenth Ordinary Assembly of the Synod of Bishops scheduled for the Jubilee Year 2000 will find the bishops talking about themselves. The theme of this important gathering is "The Bishop: Servant of the Gospel of Jesus Christ for the Hope of the World." As the preface of the *lineamenta* (the preparatory document for the Synod) points out, this assembly of the world's bishops will "celebrate episcopal communion" and "bring to a logical conclusion the recent series of synodal assemblies."

This Synod on bishops can be viewed as a conclusion to other recent Synods that have examined the vocation and mission of other components of the Universal Church. First, in 1987, there occurred the Synod on the laity which resulted in the historic document, *Christifidelis Laici* ("The Lay Members of Christ's Faithful People"). In 1990, the next general assembly dealt with the formation of priests and saw the promulgation of *Pastores Dabo Vobis* ("I Will Give You Shepherds"). Then, in 1994, the Synod fathers discussed the members of the Church committed to the consecrated life, and the Pope wrote the follow-up letter, *Vita Consecrata* ("Consecrated Life"). Now to close this circle of reflections about various roles in the Church, the bishops will reflect upon their own vocation and service.

Vocations of the Laity

While the *lineamenta* sets forth a very ambitious agenda for the assembly, I will focus here on the ministry of the bishop in relation to the lay faithful. It is an interesting topic and extremely relevant, particularly in light of the ever-expanding role of laity in the Church and the frequent misunderstandings that have accompanied its growth.

The *lineamenta* provides a summary of the current teaching of the Church on the vocation and mission of the laity in the Church and the world, and in so doing underlines the specific role the laity have in ordering the affairs of secular society toward the kingdom of God:

Their baptismal dignity which makes them participants in the royal priesthood of Christ and the special gift of the Spirit in Confirmation confer upon them a unique place in the Church community. . . . In their regard, the Church acknowledges and highlights the redemptive value of the secular character of a major part of their activity. The laity exercise their proper Christian responsibility in many areas, including family, civil life, the professional world, society, economy, culture, science, the arts, international relations, and the mass media (no. 38).

With this solid foundation, the document goes on to highlight the value of "associative groups among the laity" as a source of great richness for the post-conciliar Church. It says that these associations, "while maintaining their legitimate diversity, have to be united in their overall purpose, namely, that of a responsible sharing in the mission of the Church as bearers of the light of the Gospel" (*ibid.*, no. 40).

The document emphasizes that in relation to the laity the bishop must: (a) be the "living sign of the God who calls everyone to the one hope"; (b) ensure that the laity do not look upon their religious convictions as a purely "private affair" or shirk their responsibilities through a kind of "flight from the world"; (c) have a special concern for Catholics who "have made wrong choices in life or have 'drifted' away from the Church"; and (d) oversee the "proper formation of the laity," with a special place given to "teaching the social doctrine of the Church" (*ibid.*, nos. 41-42).

The *lineamenta* thus offers a synthesis of the role of the laity in the Church and world as well as the responsibility of the bishop in relating to the laity under his care. But what does all this mean in practical terms for the daily life and ministry of the bishop? I return to the image of the crosier mentioned above.

By Hook or by Crook

You know, of course, that the crosier has two ends: at one end a hook, at the other end a point. In tending his sheep, a shepherd sometimes uses the hook of the staff to keep the flock from drifting away. At other times, he uses the point of the staff to prod the sheep, to get them moving in the right direction. In a way, this summarizes the duties of a bishop in relating to his flock.

In other words, the bishop is a unifier and a motivator. He is, first of all, the source and sign of *unity* for the lay faithful. This function is fulfilled in many practical ways. The bishop is obliged to provide proper formation for the laity and to ensure that they have effective and sound leaders. It is the bishop's role to remind the laity of the broader Church, that is, the diocesan Church and the Universal Church, lest they become trapped in their own particular spheres of activity and lose sight of the gifts and needs of others.

Additionally, in promoting the unity of the laity, it falls upon the bishop to see that the laws and disciplines of the Church are followed so that they are not led astray by ignorance, misunderstanding, or the misdirected agendas of others. And finally in this regard, it is the duty of the bishop to foster proper respect for the various vocations in the Church—priesthood, consecrated life, and laity alike—so that these roles not become confused in theory or in practice.

Empowering the Faithful

But the work of the shepherd is not only to restrain the flock and protect it, but also to move it. In other words, the bishop also creates *vision* and *motivation* for the laity as they assume their proper place in the Church and world. This task, like the other task, has several real consequences. The bishop should be aware of the pastoral concerns of his particular Church and the secular community that surrounds it, and be willing to enlist individuals and associations to respond to those needs.

It is very important that the bishop take the initiative to recognize and affirm the good work the laity is performing in the Church and the world. It is also extremely helpful when the bishop can be personally present to these faithful people and their service, not only cheering from the sideline, but sometimes getting involved in the activity itself in ways that are appropriate and effective.

For example, at the 1998 Chrism Mass in the Diocese of Youngstown, I explained that the chrism, through the Sacraments of Baptism and Confirmation, instills new life in the faithful of Christ, and that through their service, the faithful instill new life in the world. I proceeded to single out and publicly affirm several groups of laity in the diocese who, without much recognition or support, had carried the hope of the Gospel into the world around them. I mentioned a small, but committed, pro-life group in the diocese; laity who were involved in the ever-expanding prison ministry of the Church; couples who were faithfully teaching Natural Family Planning; members of a Catholic Interracial Council who worked to build bridges among people of different races and backgrounds; and members of the St. Vincent de Paul Society who cared for the poor and needy throughout the year.

My words were appreciated, and by this simple approach, many laity of the diocese received some well-deserved recognition. They were encouraged by their bishop on that occasion to keep up the good work they were doing.

So how does a bishop relate to the lay faithful? Very simply as a pastor—a shepherd who gives his life to keep the flock together and to direct it along safe paths.

The *lineamenta* insists that if the desired renewal envisioned by Vatican II is to be achieved, much depends on the bishop: "This is an inescapable fact, since, as a result of their ministry, the bishops are builders, guarantors, and guardians of the Christian community over which, in Christ's name, they have been set as pastors" (no. 2).

Fortunately, bishops are not alone in their work. In discharging their responsibilities to the laity, bishops are blessed by the guidance of the Holy Spirit and encouraged by the conviction that

> they themselves were not established by Christ to undertake alone the whole salvific mission of the Church to the world, but that it is their exalted office so to be shepherds of the faithful . . . "according to the functioning in due measure of each single part—derives its increase to the building up of itself in love" (LG 30, quoting Ephesians 4:15-16).

It will be the goal of the forthcoming Synod of Bishops to assist the shepherds of Christ as they strive to fulfill their noble duty to build up the Church, the Body of Christ, as we together embrace the challenges and promises of the third millennium.

Most Rev. Thomas J. Tobin is the Bishop of Youngstown, Ohio, and a member of the episcopal advisory council of Catholics United for the Faith.

Chapter Six

—Standing on Solid Ground—
The Bishop as Teacher
by Most Rev. John J. Myers

People today have various notions about what it means for a bishop to teach. Very often they understand a bishop's teaching in the same way that a professor teaches, with no further distinctions.

I have had an unusual experience in this regard. A man who is a professor of communications and rhetoric at a university in the United States has taken it as a personal project to analyze my own teaching. He offers many suggestions about how I might improve my teaching, and I am sure he has many helpful things to offer. But his basic criticism is that I present people with a dilemma. In order to deal with the teaching, they must either abandon certain positions or accept and follow the teaching. He considers this to be unproductive and unhelpful. And from the point of view of the academic and intellectual climate in the United States, it is surely unusual.

Teaching in this way can only make sense if one is teaching not simply from a standpoint of personal conviction, but from a standpoint of a greater truth to which people are called. An invitation to accept God's truth is the basic responsibility of the college of bishops—with the Bishop of Rome as the head of the college—and of individual diocesan bishops for the flock entrusted to them.

Teaching with Authority

The Second Vatican Council, in its Decree on the Pastoral Office of Bishops in the Church (*Christus Dominus*), emphasizes the importance of preaching the Gospel for the ministry of bishops:

> Fortified by the Spirit they should call on men to believe or should strengthen them when they already have a living faith. They should expound to them the whole mystery of Christ, that is, all those truths ignorance of which means ignorance of Christ (CD 12).

Ours is a faith not generated by human beings. It does not find its origin in human insight and understanding, even though it can be assisted, purified, and strengthened by these. Rather, ours is a faith based on the profound and intimate self-revelation of God in Jesus Christ. It is a gift given to us. This revelation, preserved in Sacred Tradition, both written and oral, is to be preserved in the Church at all times. Those truths associated with the "deposit of faith" must also be preserved (cf. DV 7-10).

All the bishops of the world with the Bishop of Rome as its head constitute a college which succeeds the college of apostles. Just as Christ sent the apostles to teach with authority by the strength and guidance of the Holy Spirit, so bishops teach according to their office (cf. Catechism, nos. 861-62).

The Magisterium of the Church teaches with authority in various ways and at various levels. The Roman Pontiff can himself teach by virtue of his worldwide office. The college of bishops can teach in union with the Pope either when gathered in an ecumenical council or when exercising what is called the ordinary and universal

Magisterium. The latter is engaged when the Pope and the bishops of the world teach in unison on a particular point over a long period of time.

Individual bishops teach with authority when they teach by their office and in communion with the episcopal college:

> In order that the full and living Gospel might always be preserved in the Church the apostles left bishops as their successors. They gave them "their own position of teaching authority." This sacred Tradition, then, the sacred Scripture of both Testaments, are like a mirror, in which the Church, during its pilgrim journey here on earth, contemplates God, from whom she receives everything, until such time as she is brought to see him face to face as he really is (DV 7, quoting Saint Irenaeus).

Embracing the Truth

Because the Magisterium of the Church teaches with authority from Christ and with the help of the Holy Spirit, members of the Church are not free to treat this teaching as simply another opinion. All have the responsibility to accept official Church teaching according to the mode of that teaching (cf. LG 25; DV 5, 10).

In 1998, Pope John Paul II, together with the Congregation for the Doctrine of the Faith, underscored this responsibility and made it more precise in the light of the tendency by some in the Church today to minimize or even ignore their responsibility to adhere to the faith as taught by the Magisterium.[1]

---

[1] Pope John Paul II, Apostolic Letter to Protect the Faith *Ad Tuendam Fidem* (1998).

Individual bishops, especially diocesan bishops for the people entrusted to them, are to present the truths of the faith in their entirety and help apply these truths in concrete life situations. This responsibility to pass on revealed truth unchanged and uncorrupted is entrusted to the college of bishops and to individual bishops. In fact, the faithful have a right to be instructed in the full faith of the Church (cf. Catechism, no. 2037).

Bishops exercise their responsibility to teach in a variety of ways. Certainly presiding at sacred liturgy and reflecting within that context on the Word of God is a primary way. They are also charged with supervising and supporting the catechetical effort within their particular Church and also with promoting Catholic schools. Each bishop, as a member of the worldwide college of bishops, also has missionary responsibility. They are to support and participate in evangelization efforts within the diocese, but also in the broader Church (cf. AG 6, 38).

The primary ways that bishops teach together were pointed out above, namely either in an ecumenical council or by the ordinary and universal Magisterium. Bishops can also teach together when gathered in properly established councils or even in conferences of bishops. Conferences of bishops, however, do not ordinarily teach with the kind of authority about which we are speaking. Only under certain limited conditions, the Holy Father has made clear, can conferences of bishops teach in a way which is binding on the faithful.[2]

---

[2] Pope John Paul II, Apostolic Letter on the Theological and Juridical Nature of Episcopal Conferences *Apostolos Suos* (1998).

Bishops and all who preach or teach in the Church necessarily, of course, refer to their own experience and understanding. By remaining in communion with the full faith of the Church, one's individual experience is purified, expanded, and enriched. It is as though the human instrument is a sounding board for the Word of God. Believers and those invited to faith encounter the Word of God clothed in the words and actions of other human beings.

In Dialogue with the World

Today, we are addressing that sacred Word to people who are immersed in a secular culture, one that is not truly open to the transcendent and to God. The very notion of "teaching with authority" confuses people. Our age enjoys questions and new ideas and answers often with primary reference to whether a person finds them interesting rather than to whether they represent truth. Clearly minds which are so immersed must be opened up to the transcendent. Questions must be raised. They must be called beyond where they currently stand if they are to hear the saving Word.

Yet, we must address their own honest questions and concerns. We must respect their genuine dignity as children of God. We must surely respect their freedom. Dialogue properly understood is essential. But it must be honest dialogue which acknowledges the very challenging aspects of Catholic truth.

At all times and in whatever form, preaching and teaching the Word of God is a *labor of love*. It calls for great human energy and ingenuity and resources. But always the minister must keep in mind that it is Jesus

Himself who invites our sisters and brothers to faith in Him, and it is the Holy Spirit which He and the Father send who opens the human heart to that sacred Word and heals the brokenness invariably found there. The confidence manifested by those who teach the Word of God, therefore, is not an arrogant confidence based on their own knowledge or ability. Rather, it is a confidence based on the faith-inspired knowledge that God Himself is at work in the midst of their proclamation.

> Now we have received not the spirit of the world, but the Spirit which is from God, that we might understand the gifts bestowed on us by God. And we impart this in words not taught by human wisdom but taught by the Spirit, interpreting spiritual truths to those who possess the Spirit (1 Cor. 2:12-13).

Most Rev. John J. Myers is the Bishop of Peoria, Illinois, and a member of the episcopal advisory council of Catholics United for the Faith.

Chapter Seven

—Called to Holiness—
The Bishop as Sanctifier
by Most Rev. James S. Sullivan

Are you resolved to pray for the People of God without ceasing, and to carry out the duties of one who has the fullness of the priesthood so as to afford no grounds for reproach?

On September 21, 1972, Bishop Alexander Zaleski asked me that question; it was the day of my episcopal ordination. My response, rooted in Christ's love for me, was: "I am, with the help of God."

From the day I entered Holy Orders, first as a deacon, then as a priest, and, for the last twenty-seven years, as a bishop, I have tried to be faithful to the vocation of prayer. Praying for the People of God is an inseparable part of the life of a bishop. If, as the Vatican II decree on the pastoral office of the bishop states: "[bishops] have been chosen from among men and made their representatives before God to offer gifts and sacrifices in expiation of sins" (CD 15), then every bishop has a grave obligation to lead a life of genuine sanctity for the salvation of his people. Prayer is the first step in the path to holiness required of bishops. While avoiding the Donatist error that the efficacy of the sacraments depends upon a minister's virtuousness, I do know that the bishop's ability to inspire his people on the path to holiness is greatly enhanced by his own pursuit of personal holiness.

Relationship with Eucharistic Lord

The bishop's vocation of prayer originates in a personal, intimate relationship with Jesus Christ. Throughout the course of my priesthood, I have taken joy in the quiet moments I can spend with my Lord in the Blessed Sacrament. It is also in His Eucharistic presence that I take delight in praying the Liturgy of the Hours and the daily Rosary. It is with Him that I begin my day and conclude each evening. In times of difficulty and stress, Jesus Christ is my first advisor, and He faithfully awaits me in the Blessed Sacrament.

The celebration of the Mass, whether in private or in a full cathedral, is the foundation of each day. This has also been a personal goal of mine: Never pass up the opportunity to offer the Holy Sacrifice of the Mass each day. Sometimes travel or illness has made this difficult, but I have remained faithful to this goal. As Cardinal Francis George of Chicago wrote concerning the centrality of the Mass in his essay:

> The bishop, therefore, is most himself when he is at prayer, celebrating the Mass in his cathedral, surrounded by his priests and deacons, breaking open the Word of God for the holy People of God and bringing them with him into the sacrifice which unites us most perfectly to God through the Body and Blood of Jesus Christ.[1]

Some months ago, every bishop in the world received from Rome the *lineamenta* (a type of preliminary questionnaire) for the upcoming Synod of Bishops to be held

---

[1] See p. 36.

in the Jubilee Year 2000. What struck me was the Sacred Congregation's sincere interest in the personal spiritual life of the bishop. The *lineamenta* posed many questions about the bishop's ability to find time to nourish his own soul with life-giving prayer. It is obvious that these queries come straight from the heart of Pope John Paul II: If ever you have had the opportunity to witness him celebrate the sacred liturgy, you have seen that he is consumed in meditation. The prayer of the Holy Father is even more evident when one has the privilege of celebrating a morning Mass with him in his private chapel, a privilege which I have enjoyed on several occasions. In the current successor of Peter, we bishops have the forceful example of a shepherd who leads by prayer.

Agents of Salvation

As mentioned above, Vatican II affirmed the bishop's mission to offer sacrifice for sin. The bishop, as a high priest of the New Covenant, now offers not the blood of lambs and calves, but the Body and Blood of Jesus Christ for the salvation of His people. This is the chief sanctifying role of the bishop. Jesus Christ established His Church in such a fashion that the apostles and their successors would be the agents of salvation. Not just the *messengers* of salvation, but rather the very *agents* of salvation, because Christ has chosen them and now acts through them.

To carry out this overwhelming task, the bishop delegates a portion of his ministry to priests. In the large-scale world in which we live, we often lose sight of this reality. The local parish priest is there as the bishop's vicar; he is the eyes, ears, hands, and tongue of the bishop from whom the priest receives the mandate to sanctify the People of God in the bishop's name. In special communion with Christ, the Head (cf. Col. 1:18), the bishop is to reach out in charity and humility. He is to be a teacher, promoter, and exemplar of Christian perfection. He is the servant of God and the servant of the servants of God after the example of the High Priest. Moreover, the bishop's commitment to the spiritual life should inspire his priests to the point of emulation. Thus, the unity desired within a diocesan presbyterate is brought about by the integrity of the bishop (cf. PO 7).

When a priest I know was given the title of "monsignor," someone asked him what that means. He responded: "It means I have to love the Church more, work more, and pray more." This is the attitude Jesus expects of all His priests and bishops. We have been ordained to teach, govern, and sanctify. I have always understood this last characteristic to apply not only to performing the public acts of worship by which Christ dispenses grace and sanctifies His people, but also to my personal responsibility to sanctify myself.

The opening line of Saint Augustine's *De Vera Religione* ("Concerning the True Religion") states:

> The way of the good and blessed life is to be found entirely in the true religion wherein one God is worshipped and acknowledged with purest piety to be the beginning of all existing things, originating, perfecting, and containing the universe.[2]

---

[2] Saint Augustine, *De Vera Religione* (390), as translated in J.H.S. Burleigh, *St. Augustine, Of True Religion* (Chicago: Henry Regnery Co., 1964), 1.

Even though a man becomes a bishop, he, too, is a creature of God who must be humble in His presence and recognize his own need for mercy. The bishop must submit to the authority of the Church and offer absolute praise to God according to the sacred rites that have been given for our salvation.

Our Lady's Patronage

A final consideration is the example of the Blessed Virgin Mary, Queen of the Apostles and their successors. Mary was sanctified by grace from the moment of her conception so that she could give birth to the font of sanctity, Jesus Christ. As a bishop, I have often reflected upon the similarity of my vocation to that of Mary. Each of us was called to surrender entirely our will to the will of the Father. Each of us was called to be a vessel through which grace comes into the world. Each of us was called to direct the world to Christ. Like Mary, the bishop opens his mouth to proclaim: "Do whatever he tells you!" (cf. Jn. 2:5). By prayer and fidelity to the teachings of the apostles, we come to know what Christ expects of us. May the Mother of God keep each bishop in firm union with Christ, so that the bishop's ministry of sanctifying the People of God will never be frustrated by sin and division.

Most Rev. James S. Sullivan is the Bishop of Fargo, North Dakota, and a member of the episcopal advisory council of Catholics United for the Faith.

Chapter Eight

—Tending God's Flock—
The Bishop as Shepherd
by Most Rev. Raymond L. Burke

The Code of Canon Law, recalling the teaching of the Dogmatic Constitution on the Church of the Second Vatican Council, describes the office of the bishop in the Church with these words: "[Bishops] are constituted pastors in the Church, so that they are teachers of doctrine, the priests of sacred worship and the ministers of governance" (canon 375 §1; cf. LG 20).

The ministry of governance flows directly from the bishop's service of teaching and sanctifying God's flock. The bishop, who teaches the doctrine of the faith with integrity and celebrates the sacred liturgy for the salvation of God's flock, also assists and guides the flock in following Christ faithfully, whom they have come to know through the teaching of the faith and with whom they have communion through the celebration of the sacraments, especially the Holy Eucharist.

The Image of Shepherd

The Sacred Scriptures use the image of the shepherd to describe the responsibility of the apostles for the governance of the Church. Through the prophet Jeremiah, God the Father promised to place His flock under the care of "shepherds after my own heart, who will feed you with knowledge and understanding" (Jer. 3:15). Our

Lord Jesus Christ set forth for the apostles the model of
the Good Shepherd with whom He identified Himself
(cf. Jn. 10:1-5, 10-16, 27-30). Saint Peter, in his exhortation to those charged with pastoral care in the
Church, wrote: "Tend the flock of God that is your
charge" (1 Pet. 5:2).

The image of the shepherd is most fitting for the office
of governance, for it underlines the closeness of the apos-
tle to the members of the Church and the nature of his
service to them. The shepherd must be clear and direct in
guiding the flock, but he must also be loving and gentle
in asserting what is right and good, in accord with God's
law and the example of Christ. In the Prayer of
Consecration in the Rite of Ordination of a Bishop, the
principal consecrator invokes the grace of the Holy Spirit
upon the bishop-elect with these words:

> Father, you know all hearts.
> You have chosen your servant for the office of bishop.
> May he be a shepherd to your holy flock,
> and a high priest blameless in your sight,
> ministering to you night and day;
> may he always gain the blessing of your favor
> and offer the gifts of your holy Church.[1]

The whole Rite of Ordination of a Bishop is replete with
the image of the bishop as a true shepherd of the flock.

In fact, the bishop governs most of all through example and exhortation, through teaching and counsel.

---

[1] *The Roman Pontifical* (Collegeville, MN: The Liturgical Press, 1991), vol. II,
part V, no. 26.

However, when misunderstandings or abuses creep into the life of the portion of God's flock entrusted to his care, he must set forth publicly the teaching and discipline of the Church (cf. canon 392 §§1-2). In cases of stubborn refusal to conform to the Church's teaching and discipline, the bishop must apply disciplinary measures in order to restore and preserve the right order of life in the Church (cf. canon 1341).

In short, the bishop is called to imitate Our Lord Jesus Christ the Good Shepherd by offering his life for the flock confided to him. Through his pastoral ministry, the bishop humbly serves God's people, helping them to follow Christ faithfully. The Church's discipline insists that the bishop is "to show himself concerned for all the Christian faithful entrusted to his care, of whatever age, condition, or nationality they are, whether living in the territory or staying there temporarily" (canon 383 §1). Before he is ordained, the bishop-elect is asked a series of questions regarding his intentions. One of the questions is: "Are you resolved to show kindness and compassion in the name of the Lord to the poor and to strangers and to all who are in need?"[2]

The bishop is called to serve his whole flock tirelessly, without discrimination or exclusion. The bishop must govern the local Church in such a way that it expresses faithfully its unity with the Universal Church. He makes known the needs of the wider Church and encourages the people to respond generously to the call for help.

---

[2] *Ibid.*, vol. II, part V, no. 19.

Church Law as Guide for Governance

The bishop's guide in carrying out the office of shepherd is the Church's discipline which is contained in the Code of Canon Law, the liturgical books (cf. canon 2), and other Church legislation. In promulgating the 1983 Code of Canon Law, Pope John Paul II described the distinct service of the law in the pastoral life of the Church:

> [I]t is sufficiently clear that the Code is in no intended as a substitute for faith, grace, charisms, and especially charity in the life of the Church and of the faithful. On the contrary, its purpose is rather to create such an order in the ecclesial society that, while assigning the primacy to love, grace, and the charisms, it at the same time renders their organic development in the life of both of the ecclesial society and of the individual persons who belong to it.[3]

The bishop's office of governance serves right order in the life of the Church so that the Church as a body and her individual members may grow in faith and holiness of life.

Responsibility for Vocations

One of the most important ways by which the bishop fulfills his weighty responsibility for God's flock is by providing worthy priests who, by virtue of their ordination, serve in the person of Christ the Good Shepherd in every local community. The bishop is shepherd of all those entrusted to his care, but he carries out his pastoral ministry on their behalf through his coworkers, the

---

[3] Pope John Paul II, Apostolic Constitution Promulgating the 1983 Code of Canon Law *Sacrae Disciplinae Leges* (1983).

priests. Therefore, the bishop must be constantly attentive to promote and foster vocations to the priesthood, and to provide for those who respond to the call to the priesthood a sound and fitting preparation for their future priestly ministry (cf. canon 385).

At the same time, the bishop, as a loving father, must be attentive to care for those already ordained and serving God's people as their priests (cf. canon 384). He will best serve his brother priests by helping them to be constantly renewed at the source of their priestly ministry, Our Lord Jesus Christ the Good Shepherd. The renewed spiritual life of the priests fosters the unity of the priests with their bishop and with one another, which is essential to the unity of the whole People of God.

The obedience of the bishop to the Magisterium and ultimately to Our Lord Jesus Christ is the foundation of his communion with his brother bishops and the Holy Father as head of the college of bishops. Through his own obedience, the bishop sets an example for his priests, so that they may obediently exercise their ministry in the Church, in communion with their bishop, brother priests and, ultimately, Christ Himself, in whose person they act.

Consulting the Flock

As shepherd, the diocesan bishop has responsibility for the right use of the temporal goods of the diocese, so that they may serve as effectively as possible the mission of the Church (cf. canons 393, 1276 §§1-2). Although he is assisted by the diocesan finance council and the finance officer, the diocesan bishop may never abdicate his responsibility for the right use of the resources of the diocese.

In order to carry out as fully as possible the diverse pastoral responsibilities which belong to him, the diocesan bishop is assisted by the members of the diocesan curia. The diocesan curia is composed of offices dedicated to strictly pastoral activity, to the administration of temporal goods, and to judicial cases (cf. canons 469-74). It is essential that the members of the diocesan curia know the mind of the diocesan bishop and act in harmony with the direction and goals which he has set.

The diocesan bishop is also regularly assisted by important organs of consultation: the presbyteral council and the college of consultors (cf. canons 495-502), the diocesan pastoral council (cf. canons 511-14), and the diocesan finance council (cf. canons 492-94).

The diocesan synod and pastoral visitation are two ancient, proven, and solemn ways by which the diocesan bishop carries out his responsibility for governance in the Church. By the diocesan synod, the bishop receives solemn consultation from representatives of all the faithful in the diocese, so that he may apply the Church's universal law to the local situation, underline the program of apostolic life in the area, resolve problems encountered in the apostolate or in the administration of temporal goods, encourage diocesan programs of the apostolate, and correct errors regarding faith and morals (cf. canons 460-68).

Pastoral visitation is the proven way by which the diocesan bishop remains in personal contact with the flock in each of their local communities and informs the various communities in the diocese of the programs and policies set forth by the diocesan synod (cf. canons 396-98).

The Father's Heart

Through the office of the bishop, God the Father provides shepherds after His own heart, as He promised through the prophet Jeremiah. The bishop as shepherd governs the various aspects of the life of faith of the flock entrusted to his care, so that the individual members of the flock and the whole flock may grow in faith and holiness of life.

Most Rev. Raymond L. Burke is the Bishop of La Crosse, Wisconsin, and a member of the episcopal advisory council of Catholics United for the Faith.

Chapter Nine

Proclaiming
—the Good News—
The Bishop as Servant of the Gospel
by Most Rev. Fabian W. Bruskewitz

Serving the Gospel, the sublime duty and privilege of every bishop, requires that bishops, in the words of Pope Paul VI in his *Credo of the People of God*, guard, teach, explain, and spread the truth which God revealed in a previously veiled manner by the prophets and now fully by the Lord Jesus.

In his apostolic constitution *Fidei Depositum*, Pope John Paul II says, "Guarding the deposit of faith is the mission which the Lord entrusted to His Church, and which she fulfills in every age."[1] It is certain that the apostles and their legitimate successors have received from the divine founder of the Catholic Church this solemn duty, since they make up the "Magisterium" or teaching office of the Catholic Church. To be a servant of the Gospel means, first of all, loving and guarding the Good News of Our Savior in all its fullness and beauty, and then fearlessly preaching and proclaiming it. As Vatican II teaches:

---

[1] This document was published on October 11, 1992, the thirtieth anniversary of the opening of Vatican II, upon the publication of the *Catechism of the Catholic Church*.

[T]he task of giving an authentic interpretation of the Word of God, whether in its written form or in the form of Tradition, has been entrusted to the living teaching office of the Church alone. Its authority in this matter is exercised in the name of Jesus Christ. Yet this Magisterium is not superior to the Word of God, but is its servant. It teaches only what has been handed on to it. At the divine command and with the help of the Holy Spirit, it listens to this devotedly, guards it with dedication and expounds it faithfully. All that it proposes for belief as being divinely revealed is drawn from this single deposit of faith (DV 10).

Fidelity to the Gospel

The term "gospel," meaning good and welcome intelligence of some sort, was used in many ancient, pre-Christian writings. Plutarch, for instance, in his life of Pompey, wrote about a messenger arriving at Pontus with a "gospel," that is, some good news. In Christian times, however, the term has taken on a very specific meaning, a revelation of the grace of God to fallen humanity through Jesus, the divine Mediator who, through the Holy Spirit, saves us from eternal damnation. Gospel also means the narrative of the life, doctrines, death, and Resurrection of Jesus. The word "gospel" is found in the mouth of Jesus, in the writings of Saint Paul, and in many other places in the New Testament (e.g., Mk. 16:15; Eph. 1:13).

Pope John Paul II said:

[T]he bishop as a sign of compassion is at the same *time a sign of fidelity to the doctrine of the Church*. The bishop stands with his brother bishops and the Roman Pontiff as a teacher of the Catholic faith, whose purity and integrity are guaranteed by the presence of the Holy Spirit in the Church.

Like Jesus, the bishop proclaims the Gospel of salvation *not as a human consensus, but as a divine revelation.* The whole framework of his preaching is centered on Jesus who states: "I say only what the Father has taught me" (Jn. 8:28). Hence, the bishop becomes a sign of fidelity because of his sharing in the special pastoral and apostolic charism with which the Spirit of truth endows the College of Bishops. When this charism is exercised by the bishops within the unity of that College, Christ's promise to the Apostles is actuated: "He who hears you hears me, and he who rejects you rejects me, and he who rejects me rejects him who sent Me" (Lk. 10:16). Christ's promise, by guaranteeing the authority of the bishops' teachings and imposing on the faithful the obligation of obedience, makes it crystal clear why the individual bishop has to be a sign of fidelity to the doctrine of the Church.[2]

Heralds of Faith

The *Catechism of the Catholic Church*, citing Vatican II, teaches:

When Christ instituted the Twelve, he constituted [them] in the form of a college or permanent assembly, at the head of which he placed Peter, chosen from among them. Just as by the Lord's institution, St. Peter and the rest of the apostles constitute a single apostolic college, so in like fashion the Roman Pontiff, Peter's successor, and the bishops, the successors of the apostles, are related with and united to one another (no. 880, footnotes omitted).

---

[2] Ad limina address to U.S. Bishops, September 5, 1983, no. 4, as published in *L'Osservatore Romano* (English ed., Sept. 12, 1983), 3, 5.

The Catechism goes on to say that

> [b]ishops, with priests as co-workers, have as their first task to preach the Gospel of God to all men, in keeping with the Lord's command. They are the heralds of faith, who draw new disciples to Christ; they are authentic teachers of the apostolic faith endowed with the authority of Christ (no. 888, footnotes omitted).

Similarly, Vatican II affirms the role of bishops in the teaching of the faith:

> When they exercise their teaching role, bishops should proclaim the Gospel of Christ to men. This is one of the principal duties of bishops. Fortified by the Spirit they should call on men to believe or should strengthen them when they already have a living faith. They should expound to them the whole mystery of Christ, that is, all those truths ignorance of which means ignorance of Christ. They should show them, likewise, the way, divinely revealed, to give glory to God and thus attain eternal beatitude (CD 12).

Source of Unity

It is well to remember that bishops, even before being ordained and consecrated in apostolic succession as authentic teachers and interpreters of Christ's Gospel which they are obliged to serve, are, like all the faithful, believers. Until they pass from faith to vision through the doorway of death, they must constantly measure the content of their faith, as all Catholics—clerics and laity alike—must do, against the criterion of the Church's faith, the faith that was professed always by all Catholics everywhere. They must accept and be formed by the Gospel even before they teach its truths.

It is sometimes possible, but most unusual, for bishops to defect either materially or formally from the true faith. Of course, it is not within the purview of the laity to judge whether such defection occurs, but it is the serious duty of other bishops, and particularly of the Bishop of Rome, to maintain the unity of faith among bishops, with the assistance of the Holy Spirit and the abiding presence of our Redeemer within the Church that He established and promised to be with until the end of time (cf. Mt. 28:20).

Prayer for Bishops

Because of the awesome responsibilities that our bishops carry and the literally superhuman tasks that are involved in their serving the Gospel properly, and because of their most exalted dignity that they possess in human frailty, bishops always need the support and prayers of the entire Church. Saint Caesarius, the Bishop of Arles in the sixth century, said:

> [P]ray, dearly beloved, that my episcopacy may be profitable both for you and me. It will be useful for me if I preach what should be done. It will be advantageous for you if you practice what you have heard. If we ceaselessly pray for you with the perfect love of charity and you do the same for us, with the Lord's help we will happily reach eternal bliss.[3]

---

[3] Saint Caesarius of Arles, *Sermon 232*, no. 4, as translated in *Saint Caesarius of Arles: Sermons Volume III* (187-238), The Fathers of the Church Series, A New Translation (Washington: The Catholic University of America Press, 1973).

At the end of a sermon he preached in 1505, Saint John Fisher, the Bishop of Rochester in England and future martyr, after recalling that the apostles were but soft and yielding clay till they were baked hard by the fire of the Holy Spirit, prayed:

> So, good Lord, do now in like manner again with thy Church militant. Change and make the soft and slippery earth into hard stones. Set in thy Church strong and mighty pillars that may suffer and endure great labors, such as watching, poverty, thirst, hunger, cold, and heat, who also shall not fear the threatening of princes, persecution, neither death, but always persuade and think with themselves to suffer with a good will slanders, shame, and all kinds of torments for the glory and laud of thy holy name. By this manner, good Lord, the truth of thy Gospel shall be preached throughout the world. Therefore, merciful Lord, exercise thy mercy, show it indeed upon thy Church.[4]

Most Rev. Fabian W. Bruskewitz is the Bishop of Lincoln, Nebraska, and a member of the episcopal advisory council of Catholics United for the Faith.

---

[4] As quoted in T.E. Bridgett, *Life of Blessed John Fisher* (New York: Catholic Publication Society, 1890), 2-3.

Chapter Ten

—The Thirst for God—
The Spiritual Life of Bishops
by Most Rev. Charles J. Chaput, O.F.M. Cap.

More than fifteen centuries ago, Saint Augustine wrote a prayer which every bishop should have near his pillow:

> I beg of you my God,
> let me know you and love you
> so that I may be happy in you.
> And though I cannot do this fully in this life,
> yet let me improve from day to day,
> till I may do so to the full.
> Let me know you more and more in this life,
> that I may know you perfectly in heaven.
> Let me know you more and more here,
> so that I may love you perfectly there,
> so that my joy may be great in itself here,
> and complete in heaven with you.
> O truthful God, let me receive the
> happiness of heaven which you promise
> so that my joy may be full.
> In the meantime,
> let my mind think of it,
> let my tongue talk of it,
> let my heart long for it,
> let my mouth speak of it,
> let my soul hunger after it,
> let my flesh thirst after it,
> let my whole being desire it,
> until such time as I may enter

> *through death into the joy of my Lord,*
> *there to continue forever,*
> *world without end. Amen.*[1]

What appeals in these words is not their surface piety, but their deeper urgency and longing. In fact, they're filled with a yearning very close to David's in Psalm 63:

> O God, thou art my God, I seek thee, my soul thirsts for thee; my flesh faints for thee, as in a dry and weary land where no water is (v. 1).

David, who prefigured Christ, wrote from the Judean wilderness. Saint Augustine, configured to Christ in the Sacrament of Orders, wrote from a different but equally harsh kind of desert. Himself a bishop, Saint Augustine lived in a time of vast social change and sharp theological debate. And he understood from personal experience that a bishop has no hope at all to succeed as a pastor without immersing himself—losing himself completely—in God.

Man of Prayer

In every Eucharistic sacrifice, the bishop acts *in persona Christi*—"in the person of Christ"—and God made it so for a reason. Only Christ can accomplish what the bishop is called to do. Vatican II, in its Decree on the Pastoral Office of Bishops in the Church, enjoins bishops "to teach all peoples, to sanctify men in truth and to give them spiritual nourishment" (CD 2). No man can achieve

---

[1] As quoted in Dermot Hurley, *Everyday Prayerbook with the Order of Mass* (London: Geoffrey Chapman, 1980).

this on his own. So in the course of his vocation, the bishop either becomes all Christ, or all straw. He can't give spiritual nourishment to others unless he draws it from the intimate presence of God in his own spiritual life. And that happens not just through a personal habit of praying, but by his allowing God to refashion him into a man of prayer.

Every bishop is called first to be a witness to Christ among his people, not just through words—that's the easy part—but in the outline of his entire life. We tend to dwell on the "active voice" when it comes to the verbs describing the role of bishops: They teach, they preach, they govern, they guide, they correct, console, and encourage. But above all, like a good father in any family, they *must model a surrender to the demands of love, to the people they love, and to the God who is love*.

A friend once described the spiritual life in this way: Each of us is a child with an instinct for beauty, and God, who is the beauty behind all beauty, is the hidden presence we naturally sense and seek to touch. Our lives are spent reaching for that beauty. But creation is so very great, and we're so very small . . . until God stoops down to provide us with the stool to stand on, so that we can stretch out and touch His face.

The legs of that stool are faith, hope, and love—and these are what I pray God will fill me with as a spiritual father, as a pastor, as a bishop. I will tell you why.

Faith

Faith gives meaning. Man was made for a purpose; only faith provides it, and without it the soul dies. Faith is not doctrines, though these are essential. Faith is not sentiment, or knowledge, or law, though all these play a vital role in our life of faith. Faith is the certitude that God exists and loves us, because He has revealed Himself in the one vocabulary which doesn't leave much room for disagreement: His palpable presence in our lives. Bishops preach this good news. But the irony, as C.S. Lewis once wrote, is that the hardest thing to believe is that which we have just preached or defended to another. Giving the truth away leaves an empty place in the heart. And the only way to refill it, as Saint Augustine did, is to turn back to God and beg Him again for His presence. Bishops, for all the grace of their office, are just as prone to formal faith and practical unbelief as any Christian in the pew. And, history might argue, maybe more so. This is why I pray.

Hope

Hope gives joy. Every bishop sooner than later discovers that his own skills are too poor and his own sins too stubborn to be the man his people need . . . unless the Gospel is true; unless Jesus Christ is real and present in our lives. Hope sinks its roots in faith and flowers in joy. At the end of the day, there are no unhappy saints. Saint Leo the Great, who became pope not long after Saint Augustine's death and in times no better, wrote that "there is no room for sadness on this, the birthday of life." He was talking about Christmas but, since Bethlehem, we are all living in the morning of Incarnation every day. We're part of an endless birthday of life—a birthday which sets itself, in this world, against a culture of death. The task of every believer, and above all a bishop, is to be an agent of hope. This is why I pray.

Love

Finally, love gives life. All love is fruitful. *Every* person's life animated by love is fertile and creates new life according to his or her unique vocation—some in the flesh, some in the spirit, but new life nonetheless. The better we love, the more we become the hands of God, sculpting the new beauty of a new creation. Love draws us into God Himself. And from our hearts, love calls out two other virtues which depend on it: *humility*, which allows us to forget ourselves and cherish the dignity of all God's children; and *courage*, which enables us to live and speak the truth . . . not as a weapon, but as a gift. It is not enough to speak the truth. We need, as Paul wrote, to speak "the truth *in love*" (Eph. 4:15, emphasis added). This is why I pray.

The spiritual life of bishops must be driven by that hunger, thirst, and desire for God which Saint Augustine captured with such power so long ago. When we love with this intensity—as the apostles did; as every bishop is called to do—so too will our people.

Such love changed the world once. It can do so again. It will do so again.

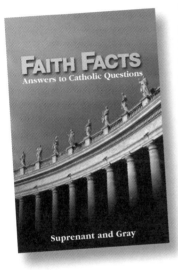

TAPE SETS AVAILABLE
THROUGH EMMAUS ROAD PUBLISHING

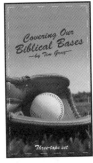

Covering Our Biblical Bases

Tim Gray goes to bat against some of the most popular Protestant objections to the Catholic Church as he provides sound, scriptural evidence for Mary's queenship, the papacy, and the ordained priesthood. Gray masterfully blends Old and New Testament passages with Jewish traditions to make these teachings come alive. (3-tape set for $19.95 + s/h.)

Restoring the Hearts of Fathers

Curtis Martin explores the challenges of marriage and family in a way that is practical and vibrantly faithful to Christ's teachings. These tapes are both lighthearted and heavy hitting, and just may be what modern men need to hear. (3-tape set for $19.95 + s/h.)

Safeguarding the Family

Philip Gray presents the practical aspects of marriage from a biblical perspective. Curtis Martin challenges men to allow Jesus Christ to transform their lives. Marcus Grodi outlines the seven essential things we must do to help our children remain faithful. (3-tape set for $19.95 + s/h.)

Winning Souls Not Just Arguments

This tape set has it all: Marian devotion, purgatory, and *biblical* teaching about justification and salvation. Curtis Martin and Patrick Madrid give you the kind of practical tips you need to answer the Church's call to evangelization. (4-tape set for $22.95 + s/h.)

(800) 398-5470
www.emmausroad.org